FOOTBALL TRAINING JOURNAL

THIS BELONGS TO:

TRAINING LOG

DATE:_____ S M T W T F S

TODAY'S FOCUS

_____
_____
_____
_____
_____

IMPROVEMENTS

_____
_____
_____
_____
_____
_____
_____
_____
_____

DRILLS/EXERCISES

NOTES/EVALUATION

TRAINING LOG

DATE: _____ S M T W T F S

TODAY'S FOCUS

_____
_____
_____
_____
_____

IMPROVEMENTS

_____
_____
_____
_____
_____
_____
_____
_____
_____
_____

DRILLS/EXERCISES

NOTES/EVALUATION

_____

_____

_____

_____

_____

_____

_____

_____

_____

_____

_____

_____

_____

_____

_____

_____

_____

_____

TRAINING LOG

DATE:_____   S   M   T   W   T   F   S

TODAY'S FOCUS

_____
_____
_____
_____
_____

IMPROVEMENTS

_____
_____
_____
_____
_____
_____
_____
_____
_____

DRILLS/EXERCISES

NOTES/EVALUATION

_____

_____

_____

_____

_____

_____

_____

_____

_____

_____

_____

_____

_____

_____

_____

_____

_____

TRAINING LOG

DATE:_____ **S   M   T   W   T   F   S**

TODAY'S FOCUS

_____
_____
_____
_____

IMPROVEMENTS

_____
_____
_____
_____
_____
_____
_____
_____
_____

DRILLS/EXERCISES

NOTES/EVALUATION

_____

_____

_____

_____

_____

_____

_____

_____

_____

_____

_____

_____

_____

_____

_____

_____

_____

TRAINING LOG

DATE:_____ S M T W T F S

TODAY'S FOCUS

_____
_____
_____
_____
_____

IMPROVEMENTS

_____
_____
_____
_____
_____
_____
_____
_____
_____
_____

DRILLS/EXERCISES

NOTES/EVALUATION

_____

_____

_____

_____

_____

_____

_____

_____

_____

_____

_____

_____

_____

_____

_____

_____

_____

TRAINING LOG

DATE:_____   S   M   T   W   T   F   S

TODAY'S FOCUS

_____
_____
_____
_____

IMPROVEMENTS

_____
_____
_____
_____
_____
_____
_____
_____
_____

DRILLS/EXERCISES

NOTES/EVALUATION

_____

_____

_____

_____

_____

_____

_____

_____

_____

_____

_____

_____

_____

_____

_____

_____

_____

TRAINING LOG

DATE:_____ **S M T W T F S**

TODAY'S FOCUS

_____
_____
_____
_____
_____

IMPROVEMENTS

_____
_____
_____
_____
_____
_____
_____
_____
_____

DRILLS/EXERCISES

NOTES/EVALUATION

TRAINING LOG

DATE:_____ S M T W T F S

TODAY'S FOCUS

_____
_____
_____
_____
_____

IMPROVEMENTS

_____
_____
_____
_____
_____
_____
_____
_____
_____
_____

DRILLS/EXERCISES

NOTES/EVALUATION

TRAINING LOG

DATE:_____ S M T W T F S

TODAY'S FOCUS

_____
_____
_____
_____
_____

IMPROVEMENTS

_____
_____
_____
_____
_____
_____
_____
_____
_____

DRILLS/EXERCISES

NOTES/EVALUATION

_____

_____

_____

_____

_____

_____

_____

_____

_____

_____

_____

_____

_____

_____

_____

_____

_____

_____

TRAINING LOG

DATE:_____ **S M T W T F S**

TODAY'S FOCUS

_____
_____
_____
_____
_____

IMPROVEMENTS

_____
_____
_____
_____
_____
_____
_____
_____
_____

DRILLS/EXERCISES

NOTES/EVALUATION

_____

_____

_____

_____

_____

_____

_____

_____

_____

_____

_____

_____

_____

_____

_____

_____

_____

_____

_____

TRAINING LOG

DATE:_____   S   M   T   W   T   F   S

TODAY'S FOCUS

_____
_____
_____
_____
_____

IMPROVEMENTS

_____
_____
_____
_____
_____
_____
_____
_____
_____
_____

DRILLS/EXERCISES

NOTES/EVALUATION

_____

_____

_____

_____

_____

_____

_____

_____

_____

_____

_____

_____

_____

_____

_____

_____

TRAINING LOG

DATE:_____ **S M T W T F S**

TODAY'S FOCUS

_____
_____
_____
_____

IMPROVEMENTS

_____
_____
_____
_____
_____
_____
_____
_____

DRILLS/EXERCISES

NOTES/EVALUATION

_____

_____

_____

_____

_____

_____

_____

_____

_____

_____

_____

_____

_____

_____

_____

_____

_____

TRAINING LOG

DATE:_____ S M T W T F S

TODAY'S FOCUS

_____
_____
_____
_____
_____

IMPROVEMENTS

_____
_____
_____
_____
_____
_____
_____
_____
_____

DRILLS/EXERCISES

NOTES/EVALUATION

_____

_____

_____

_____

_____

_____

_____

_____

_____

_____

_____

_____

_____

_____

_____

_____

TRAINING LOG

DATE:_____ **S M T W T F S**

TODAY'S FOCUS

_____
_____
_____
_____

IMPROVEMENTS

_____
_____
_____
_____
_____
_____
_____
_____
_____

DRILLS/EXERCISES

NOTES/EVALUATION

_____

_____

_____

_____

_____

_____

_____

_____

_____

_____

_____

_____

_____

_____

_____

_____

_____

_____

_____

TRAINING LOG

DATE:_____ S M T W T F S

TODAY'S FOCUS

_____
_____
_____
_____
_____

IMPROVEMENTS

_____
_____
_____
_____
_____
_____
_____
_____
_____

DRILLS/EXERCISES

NOTES/EVALUATION

_____

_____

_____

_____

_____

_____

_____

_____

_____

_____

_____

_____

_____

_____

_____

_____

_____

_____

_____

TRAINING LOG

DATE:_____ **S M T W T F S**

TODAY'S FOCUS

_____

_____

_____

_____

_____

IMPROVEMENTS

_____

_____

_____

_____

_____

_____

_____

_____

DRILLS/EXERCISES

NOTES/EVALUATION

_____

_____

_____

_____

_____

_____

_____

_____

_____

_____

_____

_____

_____

_____

_____

_____

_____

_____

TRAINING LOG

DATE: _____ S M T W T F S

TODAY'S FOCUS

_____
_____
_____
_____
_____

IMPROVEMENTS

_____
_____
_____
_____
_____
_____
_____
_____
_____
_____

DRILLS/EXERCISES

NOTES/EVALUATION

TRAINING LOG

DATE:_____ S M T W T F S

TODAY'S FOCUS

_____
_____
_____
_____

IMPROVEMENTS

_____
_____
_____
_____
_____
_____
_____
_____

DRILLS/EXERCISES

NOTES/EVALUATION

_____

_____

_____

_____

_____

_____

_____

_____

_____

_____

_____

_____

_____

_____

_____

_____

_____

_____

TRAINING LOG

DATE:_____ S M T W T F S

TODAY'S FOCUS

_____
_____
_____
_____
_____

IMPROVEMENTS

_____
_____
_____
_____
_____
_____
_____
_____
_____
_____

DRILLS/EXERCISES

NOTES/EVALUATION

_____

_____

_____

_____

_____

_____

_____

_____

_____

_____

_____

_____

_____

_____

TRAINING LOG

DATE:_____ S M T W T F S

TODAY'S FOCUS

_____
_____
_____
_____

IMPROVEMENTS

_____
_____
_____
_____
_____
_____
_____
_____
_____

DRILLS/EXERCISES

NOTES/EVALUATION

_____

_____

_____

_____

_____

_____

_____

_____

_____

_____

_____

_____

_____

_____

_____

_____

_____

_____

_____

TRAINING LOG

DATE:_____ S M T W T F S

TODAY'S FOCUS

_____
_____
_____
_____
_____

IMPROVEMENTS

_____
_____
_____
_____
_____
_____
_____
_____
_____

DRILLS/EXERCISES

NOTES/EVALUATION

_____

_____

_____

_____

_____

_____

_____

_____

_____

_____

_____

_____

_____

_____

_____

_____

_____

_____

TRAINING LOG

DATE:_____ **S M T W T F S**

TODAY'S FOCUS

_____
_____
_____
_____

IMPROVEMENTS

_____
_____
_____
_____
_____
_____
_____
_____

DRILLS/EXERCISES

NOTES/EVALUATION

_____

_____

_____

_____

_____

_____

_____

_____

_____

_____

_____

_____

_____

_____

_____

_____

TRAINING LOG

DATE:_____ **S M T W T F S**

TODAY'S FOCUS

_____
_____
_____
_____
_____

IMPROVEMENTS

_____
_____
_____
_____
_____
_____
_____
_____
_____

DRILLS/EXERCISES

NOTES/EVALUATION

_____

_____

_____

_____

_____

_____

_____

_____

_____

_____

_____

_____

_____

_____

_____

_____

_____

TRAINING LOG

DATE:_____   S   M   T   W   T   F   S

TODAY'S FOCUS

_____
_____
_____
_____

IMPROVEMENTS

_____
_____
_____
_____
_____
_____
_____
_____
_____

DRILLS/EXERCISES

NOTES/EVALUATION

_____

_____

_____

_____

_____

_____

_____

_____

_____

_____

_____

_____

_____

_____

_____

_____

_____

TRAINING LOG

DATE:_____ **S M T W T F S**

TODAY'S FOCUS

_____
_____
_____
_____
_____

IMPROVEMENTS

_____
_____
_____
_____
_____
_____
_____
_____
_____
_____

DRILLS/EXERCISES

NOTES/EVALUATION

_____

_____

_____

_____

_____

_____

_____

_____

_____

_____

_____

_____

_____

_____

_____

_____

TRAINING LOG

DATE:_____ S M T W T F S

TODAY'S FOCUS

_____
_____
_____
_____
_____

IMPROVEMENTS

_____
_____
_____
_____
_____
_____
_____
_____
_____

DRILLS/EXERCISES

NOTES/EVALUATION

TRAINING LOG

DATE:_____ **S M T W T F S**

TODAY'S FOCUS

_____
_____
_____
_____
_____

IMPROVEMENTS

_____
_____
_____
_____
_____
_____
_____
_____
_____

DRILLS/EXERCISES

NOTES/EVALUATION

_____

_____

_____

_____

_____

_____

_____

_____

_____

_____

_____

_____

_____

_____

_____

_____

_____

TRAINING LOG

DATE:_____ S M T W T F S

TODAY'S FOCUS

_____

_____

_____

_____

IMPROVEMENTS

_____

_____

_____

_____

_____

_____

_____

_____

DRILLS/EXERCISES

NOTES/EVALUATION

_____

_____

_____

_____

_____

_____

_____

_____

_____

_____

_____

_____

_____

_____

_____

_____

_____

_____

TRAINING LOG

DATE:_____ **S M T W T F S**

TODAY'S FOCUS

_____
_____
_____
_____
_____

IMPROVEMENTS

_____
_____
_____
_____
_____
_____
_____
_____
_____
_____

DRILLS/EXERCISES

NOTES/EVALUATION

_____

_____

_____

_____

_____

_____

_____

_____

_____

_____

_____

_____

_____

_____

_____

TRAINING LOG

DATE:_____ **S   M   T   W   T   F   S**

TODAY'S FOCUS

_____

_____

_____

_____

_____

IMPROVEMENTS

_____

_____

_____

_____

_____

_____

_____

_____

_____

_____

_____

DRILLS/EXERCISES

NOTES/EVALUATION

_____
_____
_____
_____
_____
_____
_____
_____
_____
_____
_____
_____
_____
_____
_____
_____
_____
_____

TRAINING LOG

DATE:_____ **S M T W T F S**

TODAY'S FOCUS

_____
_____
_____
_____
_____

IMPROVEMENTS

_____
_____
_____
_____
_____
_____
_____
_____
_____

DRILLS/EXERCISES

NOTES/EVALUATION

_____

_____

_____

_____

_____

_____

_____

_____

_____

_____

_____

_____

_____

_____

_____

_____

_____

TRAINING LOG

DATE:_____ **S M T W T F S**

TODAY'S FOCUS

_____
_____
_____
_____
_____

IMPROVEMENTS

_____
_____
_____
_____
_____
_____
_____
_____
_____
_____

DRILLS/EXERCISES

NOTES/EVALUATION

_____

_____

_____

_____

_____

_____

_____

_____

_____

_____

_____

_____

_____

_____

_____

_____

_____

_____

TRAINING LOG

DATE:_____ S M T W T F S

TODAY'S FOCUS

_____
_____
_____
_____
_____

IMPROVEMENTS

_____
_____
_____
_____
_____
_____
_____
_____
_____

DRILLS/EXERCISES

NOTES/EVALUATION

_____

_____

_____

_____

_____

_____

_____

_____

_____

_____

_____

_____

_____

_____

_____

_____

_____

TRAINING LOG

DATE:_____   S   M   T   W   T   F   S

TODAY'S FOCUS

_____
_____
_____
_____

IMPROVEMENTS

_____
_____
_____
_____
_____
_____
_____
_____

DRILLS/EXERCISES

NOTES/EVALUATION

_____

_____

_____

_____

_____

_____

_____

_____

_____

_____

_____

_____

_____

_____

_____

_____

_____

_____

TRAINING LOG

DATE:_____   S   M   T   W   T   F   S

TODAY'S FOCUS

_____

_____

_____

_____

_____

IMPROVEMENTS

_____

_____

_____

_____

_____

_____

_____

_____

_____

_____

DRILLS/EXERCISES

NOTES/EVALUATION

_____

_____

_____

_____

_____

_____

_____

_____

_____

_____

_____

_____

_____

_____

_____

_____

_____

_____

TRAINING LOG

DATE:_____ S M T W T F S

TODAY'S FOCUS

_____
_____
_____
_____

IMPROVEMENTS

_____
_____
_____
_____
_____
_____
_____
_____
_____

DRILLS/EXERCISES

NOTES/EVALUATION

_____

_____

_____

_____

_____

_____

_____

_____

_____

_____

_____

_____

_____

_____

_____

_____

_____

TRAINING LOG

DATE: _____ S M T W T F S

TODAY'S FOCUS

_____
_____
_____
_____
_____

IMPROVEMENTS

_____
_____
_____
_____
_____
_____
_____
_____
_____

DRILLS/EXERCISES

NOTES/EVALUATION

TRAINING LOG

DATE:_____ S M T W T F S

TODAY'S FOCUS

_____
_____
_____
_____
_____

IMPROVEMENTS

_____
_____
_____
_____
_____
_____
_____
_____
_____

DRILLS/EXERCISES

NOTES/EVALUATION

_____

_____

_____

_____

_____

_____

_____

_____

_____

_____

_____

_____

_____

_____

_____

_____

_____

TRAINING LOG

DATE: _____ **S M T W T F S**

TODAY'S FOCUS

_____
_____
_____
_____
_____

IMPROVEMENTS

_____
_____
_____
_____
_____
_____
_____
_____

DRILLS/EXERCISES

NOTES/EVALUATION

_____

_____

_____

_____

_____

_____

_____

_____

_____

_____

_____

_____

_____

_____

_____

_____

_____

_____

TRAINING LOG

DATE:_____ **S M T W T F S**

TODAY'S FOCUS

_____
_____
_____
_____

IMPROVEMENTS

_____
_____
_____
_____
_____
_____
_____
_____
_____
_____

DRILLS/EXERCISES

NOTES/EVALUATION

_____

_____

_____

_____

_____

_____

_____

_____

_____

_____

_____

_____

_____

_____

_____

_____

_____

_____

TRAINING LOG

DATE:_____   S   M   T   W   T   F   S

TODAY'S FOCUS

_____
_____
_____
_____
_____

IMPROVEMENTS

_____
_____
_____
_____
_____
_____
_____
_____
_____

DRILLS/EXERCISES

NOTES/EVALUATION

_____

_____

_____

_____

_____

_____

_____

_____

_____

_____

_____

_____

_____

_____

_____

_____

_____

TRAINING LOG

DATE:_____ S M T W T F S

TODAY'S FOCUS

_____
_____
_____
_____

IMPROVEMENTS

_____
_____
_____
_____
_____
_____
_____
_____

DRILLS/EXERCISES

NOTES/EVALUATION

_____

_____

_____

_____

_____

_____

_____

_____

_____

_____

_____

_____

_____

_____

_____

_____

_____

_____

_____

TRAINING LOG

DATE:_____ **S M T W T F S**

TODAY'S FOCUS

_____
_____
_____
_____
_____

IMPROVEMENTS

_____
_____
_____
_____
_____
_____
_____
_____
_____

DRILLS/EXERCISES

NOTES/EVALUATION

TRAINING LOG

DATE:_____ S M T W T F S

TODAY'S FOCUS

_____
_____
_____
_____
_____

IMPROVEMENTS

_____
_____
_____
_____
_____
_____
_____
_____
_____

DRILLS/EXERCISES

NOTES/EVALUATION

_____

_____

_____

_____

_____

_____

_____

_____

_____

_____

_____

_____

_____

_____

_____

_____

_____

_____

TRAINING LOG

DATE:_____ **S M T W T F S**

TODAY'S FOCUS

_____
_____
_____
_____

IMPROVEMENTS

_____
_____
_____
_____
_____
_____
_____
_____

DRILLS/EXERCISES

NOTES/EVALUATION

_____

_____

_____

_____

_____

_____

_____

_____

_____

_____

_____

_____

_____

_____

_____

_____

TRAINING LOG

DATE:_____ S M T W T F S

TODAY'S FOCUS

_____
_____
_____
_____
_____

IMPROVEMENTS

_____
_____
_____
_____
_____
_____
_____
_____
_____
_____

DRILLS/EXERCISES

NOTES/EVALUATION

_____

_____

_____

_____

_____

_____

_____

_____

_____

_____

_____

_____

_____

_____

_____

_____

_____

_____

TRAINING LOG

DATE:_____ **S M T W T F S**

TODAY'S FOCUS

_____
_____
_____
_____
_____

IMPROVEMENTS

_____
_____
_____
_____
_____
_____
_____
_____
_____

DRILLS/EXERCISES

NOTES/EVALUATION

TRAINING LOG

DATE:_____ S M T W T F S

TODAY'S FOCUS

_____
_____
_____
_____
_____

IMPROVEMENTS

_____
_____
_____
_____
_____
_____
_____
_____
_____
_____

DRILLS/EXERCISES

NOTES/EVALUATION

_____

_____

_____

_____

_____

_____

_____

_____

_____

_____

_____

_____

_____

_____

_____

_____

_____

_____

TRAINING LOG

DATE:_____   S   M   T   W   T   F   S

TODAY'S FOCUS

_____
_____
_____
_____
_____

IMPROVEMENTS

_____
_____
_____
_____
_____
_____
_____
_____
_____

DRILLS/EXERCISES

NOTES/EVALUATION

_____

_____

_____

_____

_____

_____

_____

_____

_____

_____

_____

_____

_____

_____

_____

_____

_____

TRAINING LOG

DATE:_____ S M T W T F S

TODAY'S FOCUS

_____
_____
_____
_____
_____

IMPROVEMENTS

_____
_____
_____
_____
_____
_____
_____
_____
_____

DRILLS/EXERCISES

NOTES/EVALUATION

_____

_____

_____

_____

_____

_____

_____

_____

_____

_____

_____

_____

_____

_____

_____

_____

TRAINING LOG

DATE:_____   S   M   T   W   T   F   S

TODAY'S FOCUS

_____
_____
_____
_____
_____

IMPROVEMENTS

_____
_____
_____
_____
_____
_____
_____
_____
_____

DRILLS/EXERCISES

NOTES/EVALUATION

TRAINING LOG

DATE:_____ S M T W T F S

TODAY'S FOCUS

_____

_____

_____

_____

IMPROVEMENTS

_____

_____

_____

_____

_____

_____

_____

_____

DRILLS/EXERCISES

NOTES/EVALUATION

_____

_____

_____

_____

_____

_____

_____

_____

_____

_____

_____

_____

_____

_____

_____

_____

_____

TRAINING LOG

DATE:_____ S M T W T F S

TODAY'S FOCUS

_____
_____
_____
_____
_____

IMPROVEMENTS

_____
_____
_____
_____
_____
_____
_____

DRILLS/EXERCISES

NOTES/EVALUATION

_____

_____

_____

_____

_____

_____

_____

_____

_____

_____

_____

_____

_____

_____

_____

_____

_____

TRAINING LOG

DATE:_____ S M T W T F S

TODAY'S FOCUS

_____
_____
_____
_____
_____

IMPROVEMENTS

_____
_____
_____
_____
_____
_____
_____
_____
_____

DRILLS/EXERCISES

NOTES/EVALUATION

TRAINING LOG

DATE:_____ S M T W T F S

TODAY'S FOCUS

_____
_____
_____
_____

IMPROVEMENTS

_____
_____
_____
_____
_____
_____
_____
_____

DRILLS/EXERCISES

NOTES/EVALUATION

TRAINING LOG

DATE:_____ **S   M   T   W   T   F   S**

TODAY'S FOCUS

_____
_____
_____
_____

IMPROVEMENTS

_____
_____
_____
_____
_____
_____
_____
_____
_____

DRILLS/EXERCISES

NOTES/EVALUATION

_____

_____

_____

_____

_____

_____

_____

_____

_____

_____

_____

_____

_____

_____

_____

_____

TRAINING LOG

DATE:_____ S M T W T F S

TODAY'S FOCUS

_____
_____
_____
_____
_____

IMPROVEMENTS

_____
_____
_____
_____
_____
_____
_____
_____

DRILLS/EXERCISES

NOTES/EVALUATION

_____

_____

_____

_____

_____

_____

_____

_____

_____

_____

_____

_____

_____

_____

_____

_____

Made in the USA
Las Vegas, NV
20 December 2021

39029854R00066